Mean Green Machine

WRITTEN BY
VIVIAN FRENCH
ILLUSTRATED BY
ANA MARTÍN LARRAÑAGA

WALKER BOOKS
AND SUBSIDIARIES
LONDON · BOSTON · SYDNEY

For Cristina and Pedro
A.M.L

First published 2001 by Walker Books Ltd
87 Vauxhall Walk, London SE11 5HJ

2 4 6 8 10 9 7 5 3 1

Text © 2001 Vivian French
Illustrations © 2001 Ana Martín Larrañaga

This book has been typeset in Century Old Style.

Printed in Hong Kong

British Library Cataloguing in Publication Data
A catalogue record for this book is
available from the British Library.

ISBN 0-7445-8302-0

Notes for Children

This book is a little different from other picture books.
You will be sharing it with other people and telling
the story together.

You can read

this line

this line

or this line.

Even when someone else is reading, try to follow
the words. It will help when it's your turn!

One bus

Toot!

One blue bus

Toot!

One new blue bus

TOOT!

One machine

Beep!

One green machine

Beep!

One mean green machine

BEEP!

One new blue bus.

One mean green machine.

One two three

Ready

Steady

GO!

New blue bus goes slow

Chug! Chug! Chug!

Chug! Chug! Chug!

Mean green machine goes fast

Vroom! Vroom! Vroom!

Vroom! Vroom! Vroom!

A hill

A high hill

A very very VERY high hill.

Mean green machine

Goes up the hill

Vroom! Vroom! Vroom!

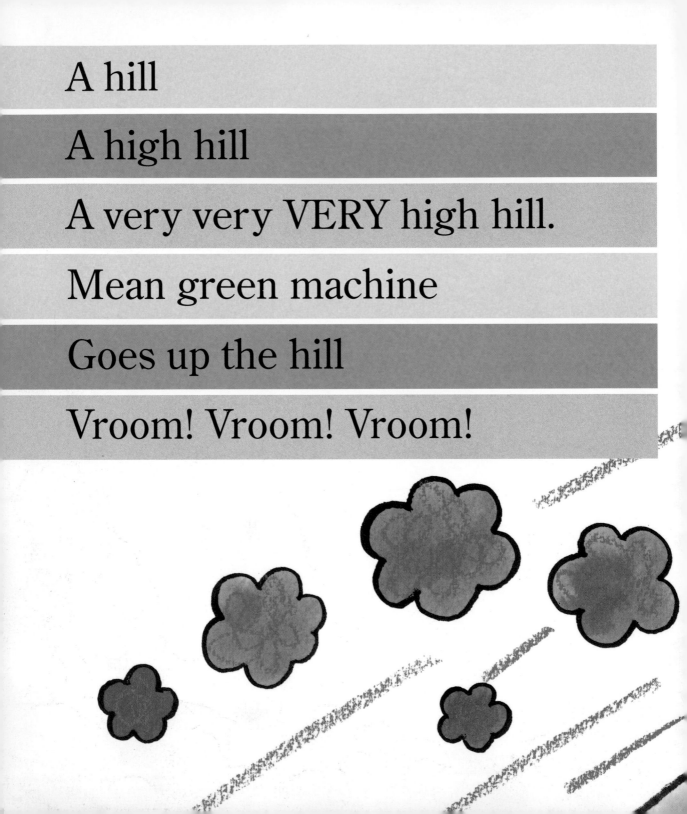

A hill

A high hill

A very very VERY high hill.

New blue bus

Goes up the hill

Chug! Chug! Chug!

Stop!

Stop at the top!

Mean green machine

At the top of the hill.

New blue bus

At the top of the hill.

One mean green machine.

One new blue bus.

One two three

Ready

Steady

GO!

Down the hill

The high hill

The very very VERY high hill.

Mean green machine

Goes down the hill

Vroom! Vroom! Vroom!

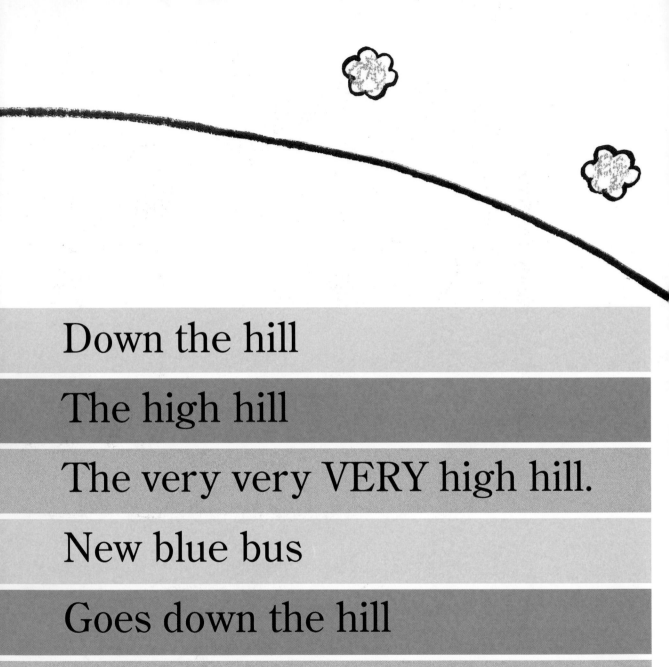

Down the hill

The high hill

The very very VERY high hill.

New blue bus

Goes down the hill

Chug! Chug! Chug!

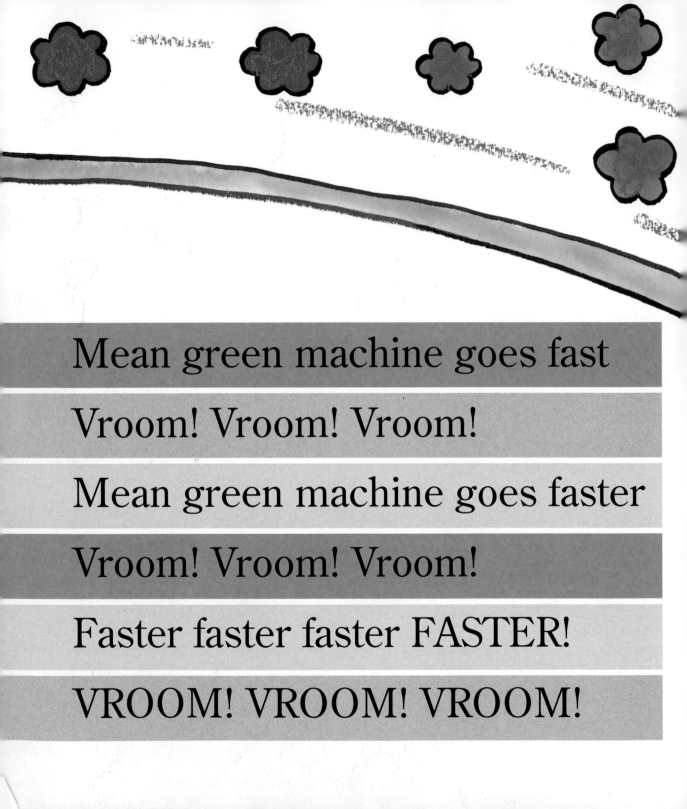

Mean green machine goes fast

Vroom! Vroom! Vroom!

Mean green machine goes faster

Vroom! Vroom! Vroom!

Faster faster faster FASTER!

VROOM! VROOM! VROOM!

BANG!!!

Green machine

Sad green machine.

Blue bus

Happy blue bus

Toot! Toot! Toot!

Notes for Teachers

Story Plays are written and presented in a way that encourages children to read aloud together. They are exciting stories, told in strongly patterned language which gives children the chance to practise at a vital stage of their reading development. Sharing stories in this way makes reading an active and enjoyable process, and one that draws in even the reticent reader.

The story is told by three different voices, divided into three colours so that each child can easily read his or her part. When there are more than three children in a group, there is an ideal opportunity for paired reading. Partnering a more experienced reader with a less experienced one can be very supportive and provides a learning experience for both children.

Story Plays encourage children to share in the reading of a whole text in a collaborative and interactive way. This makes them perfect for group and guided reading activities. Children will find they need to pay close attention to the print and punctuation, and to use the meaning of the whole story in order to read it with expression and a real sense of voice.